CROSSING THE SEA

CROSSING THE SEA

Poems by
Rachel Barenblat

ISBN: 978-1-927496-18-3

Cover art, book design and editing by Elizabeth Adams

First Edition

Published by Phoenicia Publishing, Montreal
www.phoeniciapublishing.com

For Mom

CONTENTS

ACKNOWLEDGMENTS

Many of these poems originally appeared, sometimes in earlier forms or with different titles, at the blog *Velveteen Rabbi*.

CROSSING THE SEA

Your absence has gone through me
Like thread through a needle.
Everything I do is stitched with its color.

WS Merwin, "Separation"

Learnings

That morphine is pale blue
sickly-sweet baby blue
like every cutesy sleeper
I didn't want for my infant son.

That I would feel
like a mother bird
tenderly tucking the drops
under your waiting tongue.

That the gasp and hiss
of the oxygen pump
would be both comforting
and terrible.

That when I closed my eyes
by your bedside, trying
to envision you
enrobed in light

the vision would morph
to a white Chanel suit
and I would see you
wearing your life's mitzvot

woven into a white pillbox hat
and a smart white suit
and white heels with open toes
and a cream-colored pedicure

vivacious and flirty
as a 1940s movie star
taking God's hand,
ready for the honeymoon to begin.

By the numbers

Miles I moved
to define myself

not as daughter
but as the center

of my own story:
two thousand.

Years you lived
with a diagnosis: eight.

Weeks since you died: two.
Number of times

I've reached for my phone
to show you something

—without limit.

First letter

Your grandson has taken up needlepoint.
I see you rolling your eyes. I remember
when he was five and asked to do ballet:

you demanded, "is it because you wanted
a daughter?" I snapped at you "no, Mom,
it's because he wants to try dancing."

And when he asked me to paint his nails
blue and green you averted your eyes.
My fervent hope now is that wherever

you are—the World to Come, the afterlife,
getting fabulous manicures with Shechinah
or simply resting, pain-free, in God's embrace—

all of the old life's pre-judgements
about "boys" and "girls" and what we can be
have fallen away. Look, Mom, he's taking up

needle and thread to be like me, and I'm
taking them up to be like you, to finish
the canvas you started. Isn't that what

we all do, in the end: add clumsy stitches
to the unfinished tapestry of generations?
He's trying to make something beautiful

from hard work and yarn. I told him
I'm proud of him. I told him
wherever you are, you're proud of him too.

Challah

My house smells like challah.
Three weeks ago I went through
these same motions in your kitchen.

You gave me the best gift:
you came down in the wheelchair
you hated to use, tethered

to the oxygen tank, and heard
my son sing kiddush one last time.
When we whisked the napkin

off the spiraling challah loaves
tiny sugar ants were exploring
their swirls and curves. I almost

cried, but we brushed them off
and declared the bread intact
so three generations could bless.

That night, back in bed, you said
"it's been too short, but
it's been sweet." Did you mean

our visit, or your eighty-two years?
We flew home the next morning
not knowing we would return

within a week. For days I kept
marveling, "she ate steak
at Shabbat dinner," as though

that mattered. What I meant was
you were so alive. Shabbes is coming
and I can't FaceTime with you

from the place where you are now.
You'd say "don't be maudlin."
I'm trying, but every minute

takes me farther from the one time
I baked challah for you, deeper
into this world where you are gone.

Dream

In last night's dream you laughed
about being sick, making light

of our fears. I heard your voice
but I didn't see you: I was caught up

trying to fix a garbage disposal
that wasn't working anymore.

In last night's dream I stood
in front of a room full of strangers

to say kaddish for you. I turned
every page in every book

but couldn't find the words...
Awake now, I remember the story

my chaplaincy supervisor told
about the patient who went on and on

about dysfunctional plumbing.
The punchline was, she was talking

about her own body and didn't know it.
And in my dream I focused

on the pipes, the broken housing
instead of on the laughter

that still flows. As for
my fear of forgetting the words—

you'd say I don't need them anyway.
You said once that all you want us to do

is visit your grave with a roadie in hand,
pour a splash on the thirsty earth.

I'm pouring out poems to water the soil.
We buried a box, but you aren't inside.

To the Management

I would like to register a complaint
about grief. Whose idea was this?

Even after four weeks, grief is a wave
that hits sometimes at chest height

and sends salt water up my nose.
To make matters worse, it swamps me

at the grocery store—I'm not even
at the goddamn beach. Grief is thick glass

that crushes me like a pressed flower.
Grief is the same menu over and over.

Grief is banal as a crayon drawing
by someone else's kindergartener.

I would like to exchange this grief
for something that fits me better,

in a more flattering color.
I would like to set it afire, kindled

on a bed of crumpled tissues
and return it to Sender.

Fine

Dear Mom, today I was fine
until my son played piano

and crowed "make a video, send it
to Nonni" and then his face fell.

When hospice began you told us
to stop moping. You'd tell me now

to make hay while the sun shines,
suggest that I hire a sitter

and go out with friends—
just dab a little concealer

so no one can see I've been crying.
Mom, I'm trying. But nothing

feels real without you here to see it
and I just sang my son

the lullaby I sang to you
as you were dying.

Last outing

I flew down to visit after your third fall.
Nothing felt normal, but somehow I coaxed

you into getting out of bed just once
so I could treat you to a pedicure.

You said sure, but when time came to go
just getting yourself dressed had wearied you.

You rallied, pushed your walker to the door
turned down the visor mirror and then frowned

"I can't go to the beauty shop like this."
I tried to quip, "I guess we go when we

don't yet feel beautiful," but it fell flat.
When we arrived, the bombshell: now the chairs

for pedicures were up a flight of stairs.
You hadn't gone up stairs in years. You made it

step by awful step and then collapsed
into a chair and closed your eyes. Your calves

were bruised, your tiny ankles swollen tight.
She was so gentle when she washed your feet

I thought despite myself of *taharah*,
the way we wash the bodies of the dead.

Origin story

You couldn't bear the thought of an empty nest. Then your water broke on the tennis court, ten weeks ahead of schedule. The hospital placed me in a glass isolette, in a room papered with yellow ducklings, and sent you home. When they called to say the baby wasn't going to make it, you sent Dad and the other kids to visit. You couldn't bear to meet me only to say goodbye. We always missed each other, ready for relationship too early or too late.

Uncomplicated bereavement

At the doctor's office
a questionnaire
about sadness.

I answer honestly, then
backpedal: my mother died.
This is just grief.

Later a friend gives me
the medical billing lingo:
"uncomplicated bereavement."

I almost laugh. Find me
a daughter mourning her mother
without complication.

I think of the photo
on your bathroom mirror
from what you called

the best days:
"when Dad was thin, and we
were rich, and Rachel was easy."

For years I was convinced
you wanted a different daughter,
one who stayed

in Texas, pledged
the right sorority,
married up.

We got better
at being mother
and daughter by the end.

But I hate the fear
you might have thought
I wanted a mom who wasn't you.

Letter for the end of shloshim

Dear Mom: it's been four weeks
since we sat in flimsy folding chairs
beside a gaping rectangular hole.
The morning was raw, too cold

for my son's summer-weight suit.
Someone gave him a navy-blue blanket
—the funeral home? the limo driver?—
and he curled up in it, half in my lap.

At the end, when most people returned
to their cars, he wanted to stay
and keep shoveling earth onto the box.
He brought the blanket home on the plane

and sleeps with it every night.
Maybe it feels like a last hug from you.
I haven't asked: he doesn't want
to talk about the sad things now.

You'd applaud that, but I don't know
how to live without looking back.
At the end of shiva I wrapped myself
in your monogrammed sable stole

and walked around my neighborhood,
blinking like a mole bewildered by sun.
Like my child, still wrapping himself
in the plush blanket from your funeral

carrying you with him from bedroom
to living room sofa and back again.
As I prepare to leave this first month
I'm still learning how to carry you.

Texts from the hearse

When you have a rabbi for a daughter
sometimes you get texts from the hearse.
You must have known what I was doing:
reminding myself that I still had a mother,
bracing against—well, now: not being able
to reach you to talk about purses or friends
as the cemetery's energy slowly drained.

Dear Mom, I'm wearing the same black suit
I wore to your funeral. As for purses
I'm carrying the one you gave me last year,
bright yellow like the forsythia flowers
that are curled now in hidden potential—
they still have time to bloom.

How

How can I make dinner
when you died
when dad's going to die

when someday I will bury
all of my siblings
the way we buried you?

The agony passes
but I can feel the hole
where your presence used to be

alongside echoes
of all the empty places
to come.

Kintsugi

Today a giant cardboard box arrived.
Ceramic plates that once were yours,
adorned with hand-drawn faces.

But inside the bubble-wrap
one plate's in pieces. I look
on eBay but there's no replacement.

I try to glue it, though
my son rolls his eyes: "Mom, you know
there's no repairing a broken heart."

What can I do but paint broken places
gold? I can't hide my cracks.
All I can do is make them gleam.

Beauty

At Olmos Beauty Parlor, age five,
I made a dragon from foam curlers

(from big red to small purple)
while you tipped your head back

in the shampoo chair, relaxing
into the scalp massage.

You went platinum blonde
in the sixties. Hair like that

needs maintenance. Not to mention
your nails, which were never bare.

Even the week you died
they were sleek, cream-colored.

Mom, you'd be pleased: in my 40s
I've finally found a stylist.

After your funeral, one of my brothers
gave up shaving for 30 days

(I'll bet you can guess which.)
And I went without a haircut

until the door of that first month
was closed behind me. Today

my stylist gave my hair shape
and trimmed my cuticles

and gave one nail a little sparkle
in memory of you. I emerged

with new hands, ready
to build something beautiful

in the world, ready
to hold my head up high.

Flashback

At twenty-two I wrote
about the Christmas tree

my fiancé and I decorated
in our tiny first apartment.

We had so few ornaments
we covered it in origami.

You called me in a fury.
"Where did we go wrong

raising you?" you railed.
"Sharing our family's

dirty laundry all over
the internet!" You meant

the tree, a sure sign
of my assimilation.

"How can you say that about my life,"
I yelled, and hung up.

No: I wailed that to my therapist
later. I don't remember what

I said to you. I remember
your dark certainty

that my grandfather
was rolling over in his grave.

I remember
knowing you were ashamed.

Dirty laundry

When I'm chastised
for not focusing

on happy things
as you instructed

shame swamps me,
a sunken rowboat.

Failing you again:
airing in public

the dirty laundry
of my heart.

Why persist in
feeling so many

feelings, especially all
the ugly ones—

grief that lasts
for hours, leaving

me gasping, spent
on the shore?

Wouldn't everyone be
happier if I

stopped?

Goldfinch

Mom, I bought a new piece of art
I wish I could show you.
There's a goldfinch, encircled
by crocheted six-pointed stars.

It makes me think of home,
of nest, of tradition's weave
that comforts me. I wonder
if you'd note the bird's alone.

Yes, I feel alone in grieving.
Maybe we all do, in the end—
even when a crowd gathers
for a memorial like yours.

Surely as Pesach approaches
everyone in the family feels
your absence, like the empty space
surrounding this one little bird.

with gratitude to Heather Robinson

Challah, take two

Winter vacation: snowy day
with nightfall too soon

and no playdate in sight, I said
"let's bake challah!"

"Can you make it round
like Rosh Hashanah?" he asked.

Instead I tried a six-branched spiral
meant to evoke the returning sun

(though my son saw a star
of David there instead.)

When it emerged from the oven
golden and gleaming

he gasped, and after motzi
proclaimed it "so much better

than what we buy at the store,"
and that sealed it:

the next Friday I found a way
to start the dough

when I poured his cereal,
to knead it while he watched

YouTube before school, to pop
home at lunchtime to shape...

I would have told you this story
that last Shabbat of your life

but that morning was a fog
of morphine and anxiety

and when you emerged that evening
miraculous in your wheelchair

it wasn't the right time.
I should have known

there wouldn't be another.
But I can tell you now

that even in weeks when grief
is more than I can bear

there is comfort in kneading
this silky egg dough,

singing healing songs for all
who will eat, for all who ache.

Birthing

Four days before the end.
Morphine under your tongue.

You kept asking,
"When will it stop hurting?"

Reminded me of labor:
how the contractions kept coming.

I pleaded, "I can't do this."
When the epidural brought relief

I apologized to the nurses
for being boring.

How we learn to say sorry
for what's not ours to carry...

But Mom, I still carry this:
I'm sorry I said no

to your presence
when my son was born.

I wanted it to be intimate,
"just the two of us."

I understand now: it hurts
to be far away

when someone you love
this much is suffering.

You could have
witnessed the moment

when they placed him
wide-eyed on my chest.

You wanted so much
of my heart.

I just wanted
to cut the cord.

We fought

Because I didn't like aerobics. Because I wrote revealing poetry. Because I thought you were prejudiced. Because I knew you were frivolous. Because I didn't like the right boys or befriend the right girls. Because I rolled my eyes at you calling blue cheese "bad" when you really meant "fattening." Because I said Palestinian as though they were people. Because I married a non-Jew. Because I wrote too much about me and not enough about Israel. Because you thought when I stopped wearing contact lenses, it was because I wanted to be more like his mother than like you. The truth is, in those days I did want that, but I didn't want to admit that everything really was about me and you.

New friend

Today two women told me stories
about their dead mother.
I imagine the two of you
meeting at a mixer
for newly-arrived souls.

In my vision you're both
young again, glamorous,
coiffed and gleaming.
You're carrying copies
of the handbook to the afterlife

but you'd rather sip vodka
and make a new friend
than read. That's okay:
you'll learn the ropes.
How to visit our dreams

and tell us everything
you couldn't say in life
or maybe it was we
who couldn't hear, but
Mom, we're listening now.

Jetlag

Pitcher and basin
at the door
when we return
from the cemetery.

The first hours
are like jetlag,
soul catching up
with the body.

Nothing feels familiar.
Your house, but
not your house.
The silver pitcher—

I keep thinking
of South Pacific,
"wash that man
right out of..."

You would have
sung with me.
But this door
isn't yours anymore.

How long does
it take to
release from your
body's dead shell?

When you wake
in the afterlife
is it like
a new timezone?

Is there a
pitcher at the
threshold of the
world to come

so you can
wash this life
and its sorrows
away?

Another

This time the day was wet and raw, like your funeral was.
This time there were two daughters grieving, but I wasn't

one of them. Except I still am, sometimes. It depends
on what song comes on the radio, what phase the moon.

Today when we read psalm 23 aloud I remembered my sister
leaning over to whisper, "'my cup runneth over,' Mom used to

say that all the time!" It made me smile. You
make me smile, even at a funeral that reminds

me of yours, reminds me — everything reminds me —
of you.

Request

There's a lot of death
in those poems, you say to me.
How about something
a little brighter?

Isn't it spring yet where you live?
Talk to me about tulips
like the ones that nod
in bright even rows down Fifth Avenue.

Talk to me about
department store windows,
or that lime-green bag
you took from my closet.

Your friend who's divorcing:
what's her new house like?
Tell me about the red buds
on the tips of the maple,

or my grandson's new haircut
that makes him look thirteen.
Tell me something about the world
that will make me miss being alive.

Trivia

The envelopes would arrive at random:
filled with clippings, sometimes

highlighted in yellow, with a Post-It
reading "Trivia From Mom." Dear Mom:

here's some trivia from the living.
I refilled a prescription today, and

picked up the dry cleaning. I've been
wearing your cashmere shawl

on cold days—believe it or not
we still have those. My son

practices the Four Questions nightly
before bed, earnest and sweet.

Do you remember typing them
on your IBM Selectric for me,

transliterated—one of my brothers
must have sung them to you —

so I could sing them before I knew
Hebrew? You'd be proud of him.

For a while I was afraid
we'd left one of his dress shoes

in Texas at your funeral, but
it turned up at his father's house.

Now I can go hours at a time, forgetting
that it hurts that you're gone.

Dance class

Parent observation night
at the dance school.

I caught my son with my camera
in an idle moment

running his hands through his hair.
He looked like a teenager.

When I was nine
I still threw my arms

around your neck, but by fourteen
I kept my distance.

We no longer spoke
the same language. Maybe

I'll be spared that: we're not
mother and daughter, he and I.

But if he grows
to mistrust me, I hope

I live long enough
to make it to the other side

as you and I made it
to the other side

even though I know
you'd be relieved to know

he's not the only boy
in his dance class this year.

Bedtime

Tonight at bedtime
my son weeps:

his favorite lovey
got left behind.

He keeps searching,
saying "Sealie? Sealie?"

My brown bear
my red dog

are long gone,
but I know

how it feels
to yearn helplessly

from afar. When
we invoke angels

surrounding, we ask
look after Sealie

the same way
that last night

I asked them
to accompany you.

This earth our home

When the house lights went down
I started to cry. It's just
a third grade concert—songs

about "this earth our home"
with canned accompaniment
and elementary school kids

fidgeting on the risers—but
you'd have loved it.
His whole life you were too sick

to travel to see him shine.
It wouldn't have occurred to him
to expect you there, but

I would have texted you a video
the minute I got to the car.
You'd have watched it later

when you woke up, when you felt
up to checking your phone.
You would have sent a string

of celebratory emojis. You'd have
laughed that he knows already
how to make a mike stand taller,

praised his stage presence...
I wiped my eyes furiously, hoping
no one noticed the ridiculous mom

in the second row who was moved
to tears by songs about recycling.
This is how I send you video now,

Mom: these poems I don't know
if you can hear from where you are,
this earth no longer your home.

My third bicycle

My first bicycle was hot pink.
When I was eight and skipped PE
for weeks on end you hired Coach
to tutor me. She taught me

how to catch a frisbee,
not flinch from a softball,
ride a bike without training wheels.
My second was electric blue

and I rode it barefoot around
the curves of Contour Drive
past magnolia and honeysuckle
with wind in my hair.

When I grew hips I put the bike away.
I felt like a galumphing goose
next to you, perfect petite
size zero sparrow.

By college when my boyfriend
invited me to bike across Nantucket
I demurred, sure he wouldn't
want me if he saw me huff and puff.

But I remember your red Schwinn
with a tiny seat bolted to the back
for me. I remember the freedom
of skimming along Contour

once I was old enough to go
further than you could see.
Mom, today I bought a bicycle.
It's black and solid, German,

a middle-aged woman's bike.
When I go riding with my son
I'll say a shehecheyanu. Maybe
I'll feel you perched behind me.

They say the body never forgets
these old motions. I wouldn't mind
forgetting how to resent
every ounce and inch

that made me not like you.
From where you are now
can you teach me how to thank
this clunky, sturdy frame?

Before Pesach

The year your mother died
just before Pesach

I remember my grandfather
at the seder.

He had aged, inexplicably.
He looked lost.

But I don't remember you
that year: were you

grieving, did you struggle?
I was a teenager

and we didn't communicate
much, you and I.

I hope someone asked you
how you were.

I hope someone told you
it was okay

to grieve your father's
diminishment,

to feel her absence like
a missing limb.

I hope there was comfort
in the words, the wine

the songs, the soup—
how though the ground

of your being had shifted,
the seder hadn't changed.

Four questions

Will you and your parents sit down to seder on high
on the night when we sit down to seder below?

Who sings the Four Questions, the person in the family
most newly-arrived to the afterlife?

Will you thank the Holy One, Blessed Be God
for lifting you with mighty hand and outstretched arm

out of the Mitzrayim of your bodies,
your illnesses, cancer or dementia or broken-down lungs?

Will you dip parsley in salt water, or are the tears
you cried in this world enough to last you for eternity?

No answer

Dad says he visits you
at the cemetery
every day, except
Saturdays when the gates
are closed. (Has

grass begun to grow?
I don't ask.) We agree
you wouldn't care
about the words of kaddish
but it's what we know

to do. He says he's
mad at you for dying
asks again and again why
an incurable lung condition.
I look away.

14 Nisan

Matzah balls simmer
in home-made broth.

Your wedding silver
gleams on the tables.

Pesach is almost here
but I can't show you.

Last night's chametz
burns in a paper bag.

Your earrings

For first seder I'm wearing
your earrings, turquoise and onyx.

Will they act as microphones
transmitting wirelessly to olam ha-ba

every compliment on your jewelry,
the sound of your youngest grandson

singing the questions high and clear?
In return maybe they'll whisper to me

a request to nudge my father on this night
of all nights not to wear bluejeans.

Maybe they'll let me hear an echo
of your fingers at a piano on high.

Songbird

In the open window
as we began seder.

Between the readings
a fountain of birdsong.

That's your mother,
someone said, hushed.

I called us to silence.
Can everyone hear—

I think even the skeptics
felt you there.

What was it like
to visit us in that tiny body

gilding the room with song
we could almost understand?

Plates

Your Pesachdik dishes lived
in cartons on a high shelf,
strictly for the Dallas cousins.
Yours were plain white.
Some of mine are red,
gleaming like polished apples.
Others are hand-me-downs
in melon and aqua and blue,
a gift from another mother
who reached out as I joined
this motherless daughter club...
Did you wonder
why I've reclaimed
traditions you and Dad
were glad to discard—
did you shake your head
at this pendulum swing
of generations? Still,
you'd like my table this week,
bright as your nail polish,
vivid as a Fiesta parade.

Stars

In your filing cabinet you left
notes for your obituary.

At summer camp you played
the doxology on accordion.

You were proudest of
your junior lifesaving certificate.

You wished you'd learned
to tapdance, or written a book.

You included for us a list
of loves: dad, of course.

Also travel, a good party,
Judaism and your children,

your nutritionist guru,
the Big Dipper, the moon.

On Nathan J. Pritikin
we part ways. I'm likelier

to emulate Samin Nosrat
scattering Diamond Crystal salt

by the handful (sorry
Mom) but I love

that you loved the moon
enough to mention her, and

the other stars you steered by
still show me the way to shore.

Crossing the sea

As you
lay dying
you gasped
"help me."
How terrifying
to let
your lungs
stop breathing
to trust
that you
would continue
even after
your body
had ceased.
To step
into waves
that crested
so high
and know
the waters
would part.
To feel
deep in
weary bones
that from
narrow straits
expansiveness beckoned,
that redemption
was waiting
on the
far shore.

I don't mind

Today someone asked how I am
and I said fine and meant it.

Maybe I'm growing accustomed.
Maybe all those years of bracing

for your death paid off.
Maybe it's just the sunshine.

It's easier to be honest now
than it was when you were alive.

I don't have to worry
that I'm disappointing you.

And if I believe you hear me
then you're listening no matter what.

I know this ease won't last.
I'll see someone who looks

like you, a mother
and daughter with heads close...

I can't even think about
all the occasions to come.

But right this minute
with the trees leafing out

I know you're dead
but I don't mind.

Field trip

You walked through my dream last night
as a crowd of family crossed a hotel lobby.
Your blonde hair blown-dry and styled,

full face of makeup, earrings gleaming.
"You look great," I said, and you beamed
as though you knew the secret: you're not

in this world anymore. Was it a field trip
to visit the living? I greeted your parents,
gone thirty years. And then I was alone.

I seized my phone to call a friend to tell
the tale. "Next time, ask her for a bracha,"
he suggested. Waking, I thought: what would

you say? In life you would have laughed, or
said you don't know how to give a blessing
but maybe in the afterlife you're less afraid.

Or maybe you'd repeat exactly what you said
in life: make hay while the sun shines.
This life is too short. Don't miss it.

Mother's day

It's a year of firsts
and most of them hurt.

Hallmark doesn't sell a card
designed to be burned

so smoke can ascend
to reach the afterlife.

And why didn't I save
every card you ever sent me

so I could reopen them now?
I miss your handwriting.

I kick myself now
for every deleted voicemail.

Futility claims my heart.
Earth thuds onto the wooden box.

Peonies

After your mother died
you used to visit her
on her birthday

with flowers,
Texas yellow roses
you'd leave on her grave.

Were they her favorite
or just local color?
I wish I'd asked.

You loved peonies best:
their big, blowsy
spectacular faces

too tender to grow
in the hot south
where you were planted

but you knew
the best florists
would have them.

I'm too far to visit
and anyway you're not
there in the ground.

For your birthday
I put peonies
on my dining table.

The tight buds stand
straight like
young ballerinas.

The bigger blossoms
bend over,
already flirting

with the fragrance
of decay.

Ring

It's a simple circle
of pink coral, set

mid-century modern
in silver and gold.

There's a spiral
of tape on the bottom,

wound around and around
to shrink the band.

Most of your rings
had that, artifact

of fingers growing thinner
with illness and age.

Today my sundress
is navy and aqua,

turquoise and lime,
banded with coral

to match the ring
that used to be yours.

I wish I'd asked you
about its origins.

Look, Mom, I'm
wearing colors. I'm

emerging from mourning,
from winter's long grasp.

Gone

Three months later
I still dream of
tearfully telling Dad
"I'm so worried
about Mom, I'm
so afraid," and
then I wake
and soothe myself
that it's over,
you're gone, you're
not suffering anymore.

Pedicure

I got a pedicure the day you died.
I was numb and shocky, couldn't bear
to bury you without looking as good
as I knew you'd have wanted me to be.
In the chair I blurted out, "I'm going
to my mother's funeral." Today
I took that polish off my toes, replaced
with periwinkle, luminous and bright
like your big string of pearls you do not know
are mine now that you're gone. I can't text you
the nail polish emoji as a way
of showing where I am. But hi, Mom, from
the temple of appearance, holy place.
I close my eyes. I almost find you here.

Revelation

The night before Shavuot
I fall asleep hoping
for revelation.

I dream you give me
a necklace: long chain
with a cluster of charms.

Some are golden plates
engraved with the words
we'll say about you

at your funeral and shiva.
We both know it's coming.
I ask you before you go

to give me my name again.
We stand in a vast shower
—warm water flowing,

like a mikvah, like
the chevra kadisha
washing the dead clean—

and you say my name
and I hold you
while you weep.

In your shoes

When I shot up like a weed our feet
stopped matching. Our tastes
diverged too: once I moved out
I chose Docs, clunky Mary Janes.

When you got sick your shoes
languished, replaced by scuffs
and slippers. Two days after
we buried you, your daughters

and granddaughters gathered
in your walk-in closet
for a different kind of memorial.
I chose scarves and beads,

purses and pocketbooks. Didn't
bother with your shoes, those rows
of gleaming heels in leather
and lucite: like Cinderella's

step-sisters, I would've needed
to chop my feet. But one pair
of open-toed sandals beckoned.
Against all odds they fit, but

February is winter here. They went
on a shelf in my closet to wait.
Mom, last night we shared shoes
again. Were you watching as

I walked circles around the house,
relearning how heels swing my hips
playing dress-up in my mother's
shoes, now my own?

Blackbird

My son's dance performance opens
with a song you used to play.

I weep for how you rolled these chords.
I can still hear you singing

"I need someone to love and
understand me," the way you'd slow

for emphasis on "light the light,
I'll be home late tonight..."

But you won't be. Not with us.
Dare I hope the world to come

feels like home in all the ways
this world sometimes doesn't?

Now do you feel cherished
in all that you are?

Sun

Best hours for sun: ten until two.
You taught me that, sunbathing
on the flat woven chaise by the pool
straps pulled down so you wouldn't mar
any off-the-shoulder blouse
with lines. No one thinks like that
anymore. Here and now even boys
don't swim topless, exposing chests
to the depradations of our star, but
when I walk to the condo pool for a dip
I still notice whether or not I'm in
the good tan window. And later
in the shower when I see my forearms
darker against the soft pale flesh
of my belly, I feel at home in my body.
I don't look like you. But
after an afternoon spent dipping
into cool aqua waters festooned now
with tufts of fluff from cottonweeds,
my warmed skin comforts my touch
the way yours used to do.

Watch me

"Watch this, Mom, watch me."
My son jumps into the pool,
surfacing to ask "was that

a perfect pencil dive?" Or
"look at this, do I look
like a dolphin," wiggling

through the water, "or more
like a whale?" breaching
and landing with a splash.

If I don't witness, it's
as though it didn't happen.
Sometimes I watch, hungry

for every instant of his
nine-year-old summer, glimmer
of sun-sparkles on the water

and maybe a popsicle after
with hair still dripping wet.
Sometimes behind my shades

I want to roll my eyes: kid,
I can't be there your whole life
to see every move you make.

But what else are these poems
if not me calling out to you
watch this, Mom, watch me?

Chrysalis

On my Italian parsley plant
a fat green stripey caterpillar.

It's a black swallowtail
in fourth instar, readying

for its chrysalis. Unlike
the monarch, predictable

in its cycle of rebirth, these
take an indeterminate time

encased in green or brown
before emerging wet-winged.

Growth has its own pace, can't
be hurried. How do they know

when they're ready to shed
what's protected them

and open, tender, to a world
waiting for them to soar?

Postcard

This is a postcard—
oversized, five by seven
and glossy. On the front
a photo of my garden:
look, the half-dead bushes
are gone, and the tangle
of wild mint and weeds.
In their place
tall purple astilbe,
silver-leafed brunnera,
a hydrangea, periwinkle
and columbine, shasta daisy.
On the back I'll write
that the sharp scent
of fresh mulch wakes
me like a shofar. All
around town tractors are
cutting tall grass, turning
summer's verdant beauty
into something sustaining
for when all this life
is gone.

Return

Not sure what I fear more:
that your house will feel the same
or that it won't. No more wheelchair
or hospital machines, but

the books in the library will still
be arranged by color, abstract
modern art constructed from their spines'
gradations. The heavy crystal bowls

of roasted nuts for cocktail hour
will still adorn the living room
where you used to hold court with
vodka soda and lime in hand, where

you let us take a family photo
that last Shabbat. I was shocked
you let us bring out the camera:
your hair was wild, unwashed.

You smiled as though nothing hurt.
You knew it was our last chance. Mom,
I don't know how to visit a Texas
that doesn't have you in it.

You're not there anymore. You're
not anywhere. But I want to believe
you're watching. Not all the time,
but maybe you feel a tug

when I'm thinking of you. Maybe
you were there when I went shopping.
I bought a dress for the trip.
It's deep yellow, like a loquat,

like your lacquered kitchen cabinets.
I chose it to show off your necklace.
You'd like it because it's bright,
it's vivid, like something that's alive.

Hair

The alligator clips
for holding a hank of hair
while the rest is blown dry

wait patiently
for you to return
and need them again.

In your last years
you joined the ranks
of little old ladies

who let the beauty shop
wash and style.
Like your mother used to.

I always thought
they needed the bowl dryers
to set their curls.

I never understood
it was because arms
couldn't reach anymore, or

ports or open wounds
couldn't safely handle
the sluice of a shower.

I didn't know
how much I'd miss
your blowdryer's hum.

Star light

Mom, tonight
after I got
the kid to bed
I stepped outside

onto the balcony
—the air cool
without a robe
already, late

August preparing
to give way—
and the Big Dipper
gleamed above me,

and Cassiopeia.
I forgot to say
"Star light, star
bright," but

God knows
all the things
I wish for,
including

you listening
for these missives
lofted skyward
for you.

Now

Suddenly the two stately trees
outside my window are shot through

with sprays of gold. My heart rails
against the turning season

like a child resisting bedtime, but
the trees hear the shofar's call.

Come alive, flare up, be
who you are: let your light shine!

The katydids and crickets sing
the time is now, the time is now.

The last time I visited you
I said "it's okay if you're ready

to go." My heart railed against
your dying, but after one last burst

of color you were ready to rest.
This year the trees' razzle-dazzle

speaks to me in your voice: be here
while you can. Drink every drop

of daylight. And when night falls,
it's full of stars: don't be afraid.

First day of fall

Mom, I'm on my mirpesset
on the first day of fall.
You loved that word—
a little taste of Jerusalem

or Tel Aviv. Two of the zinnias
my son planted last spring
have sent up new buds, like
dancers reaching toward heaven

with palms outspread.
They're trying to bloom
once more before first frost.
I don't think there's time,

but who am I to say I know
when death will come?
All morning I've been practicing
Torah in the golden melody

of the season. Last year
you watched holiday services
from your bed, Facebook Live
on the iPad propped on your lap.

From olam ha-ba I expect
you'll have better picture
and clearer sound. I wish
I could feed you honeycake.

I wish I could sing for you
and know that you hear me.
I don't want to be starting
a year that never had you in it.

Recipe

The year your mother died
I was living off-campus
for the first time.

Rosh Hashanah approached:
I called you for recipes.
I didn't know how to cook, but

I roasted cornish hens
and honeyed carrot coins
and assembled my housemates

around a table covered
with a bedsheet because
I didn't own a white tablecloth.

As this first Thanksgiving
without you draws near,
I'm emailing my sister

and scouring the internet
for a recipe that looks
like the mango mousse

you always made. It's a relic
of the 50s when your marriage
was new. I don't think

I've ever bought Jell-O
or canned mango before, and
I don't own a fluted ring mold

but when my spoon slices
through creamy sun-gold yellow
it will taste for an instant

like you were in my kitchen,
like you're at my table,
like you're still here.

In this place

You're sick, but
still offering opinions
on which cut of trousers

best suits me. You promise
a pair of new boots, stylish
as yours, before you go.

Then you're dead, and
I roam your closet
(Narnia-sized, infinite)

with empty hands. But look:
on a countertop, the boots
you promised, in my size.

I wake laughing.
You're nine months buried
and still giving to me.

Winter solstice

"Just a few more days," you said,
"until the days start getting longer."
And I thought: I didn't realize
you counted them too, eager
for the satisfaction of knowing
that every day there is more light.
What else did we have in common
that I never bothered to know?

Chanukah gift

The closet holds
picture frames, half-empty
boxes of stationery,

pillows and blankets
for the guest bed. Tucked
amid all of these, a small box

emblazoned Priority Mail,
addressed in your hand,
postmarked two years ago.

It fell behind the quilts
and the crates of journals
until today.

As I slice open the packing tape
I can barely breathe. Inside:
a letter you wrote to my son

for the last night of Chanukah,
and some old coins—a poem
and gelt, though I know

what here is truly gold.
Your words, your memory—
the oil that keeps on burning.

On the shortest day

I sit in the quiet.
I leaf through
your cookbooks.

I remember
how you loved
the beauty shop's bustle.

When night falls
I sing my way
through the door.

I want to say
look, Mom, we made it.
But you didn't.

You aren't struggling
anymore to breathe
as night closes in.

A year ago

A year ago you kept falling. Bloodied from landing, bruised as though beaten. Dad couldn't lift you, so one night you slept on the carpet until morning. Did you know your children were scheduling frantic conference calls? There was no knowing how much worse it might get. When you consented to hospice, you texted us, "if my decline troubles you, have your doctor prescribe a happy pill." I laughed until I cried. A year ago you were still alive. This month I keep saying that, like a mantra. Soon I'll never be able to say it again.

Pebbles

I know I must have talked with you
after unveilings for relatives

or friends, but I don't remember
what you had to say. Probably

we talked about shopping or haircuts
or Shabbes dinner, what Marie Howe

called "what the living do."
When you drove out of a cemetery

you moved on, but part of me still
hasn't left where we buried you.

Soon we'll gather to bless the slab
that marks the spot. Did you know

the tradition that says we stop
saying kaddish after eleven months

because only wicked souls require
a full year of kaddish to ascend

and we wouldn't want to imply
you weren't righteous? I think

you'd laugh and say whatever works
for us is fine by you, then ask

where we're going for lunch after
and what kind of shoes I'm planning.

Almost eleven months now I've been
writing to you, each line a monument

to memory. These poems,
the pebbles I leave on your stone.

The weather

Things I can't know,
a partial list: how cold
the cemetery will be this time

how bruised my heart will feel
—or not—and most of all
would you wear sandals?

I don't think the dead
pull climate strings, but
if it were up to you

you'd want Texas to put on
her prettiest face
when we remember you.

You'd want our grief
to melt like thin ice
in morning Texas sun.

Tether

These letters, kite-string
or umbilicus: do they
tether you? When I
stop writing will you
dissolve, a water droplet
rejoining the flowing stream?
Maybe I'm the one
tied to what was,
not willing to disentangle.
When I wasn't looking
this year changed me.
Still homesick sometimes, but
I've learned to sleep
in this strange bed
where sometimes, I know,
I will see you
in dreams. Gone but
still here. Almost enough.

The far shore

This is how the year ends.
We've carried your memory, and now
we dedicate this stone
on the far side of the sea.

We've carried your memory.
Now we look back
from the far side of the sea,
our footsteps washed away.

Now we look back
and blink, disoriented,
our footsteps washed away.
The waves are gentler now.

We blink, disoriented.
I still talk to you.
The waves are gentler now
when I greet your photos.

I still talk to you
in every room
when I greet your photos
as though you were here.

In every room
questions I wish I'd asked
(as though you were here.)
I remember your voice.

Questions I wish I'd asked:
how do we live without you?
I remember your voice.
I don't want to let go.

How we live without you:
we dedicate this stone.
I don't want to let go.
This is how the year ends.

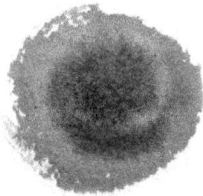

ABOUT THE AUTHOR

Rachel Barenblat, named in 2016 by *The Forward* as one of America's Most Inspiring Rabbis, is a rabbi and spiritual director. She is a founding builder at Bayit: Building Jewish and serves as spiritual leader of Congregation Beth Israel (North Adams, MA).

She is author of five previous book-length collections of poetry: *70 Faces: Torah Poems* (Phoenicia Publishing, 2011), *Waiting to Unfold* (Phoenicia, 2013), *Toward Sinai: Omer Poems* (Velveteen Rabbi, 2016), *Open My Lips* (Ben Yehuda Press, 2016), and *Texts to the Holy* (Ben Yehuda, 2018). In 2019 she edited *Beside Still Waters: A Journey of Comfort and Renewal* (Bayit and Ben Yehuda), a volume for the mourner's path.

Since 2003 she has blogged as The Velveteen Rabbi, and in 2008, *TIME* named her blog one of the top 25 sites on the internet. Her work has appeared in *Lilith*, *The Texas Observer*, *The Forward*, and anthologies including *The Bloomsbury Anthology of Contemporary Jewish American Poetry* (Bloomsbury), *The Women's Seder Sourcebook* (Jewish Lights), and *God? Jewish Choices for Struggling with the Ultimate* (Torah Aura), among other places.

She has taught courses arising from the intersection of the literary life and the spiritual life for Bayit, the Academy for Spiritual Formation, the National Havurah institute (where she was digital Liturgist In Residence in 2020), and Beyond Walls, a writing program for clergy of many faiths at the Kenyon Institute.

Rachel lives in western Massachusetts with her son.

A NOTE ON THE TYPE

The interior text typeface is Adobe Garamond Pro, designed by Robert Slimbach in 1989 as an interpretation of original roman and italic faces by the French type designers Claude Garamond (1505-1561) and Robert Granjon (1530-1590). The display typeface is Helvetica Neue (Light Extended), designed in 1983 by the German typographic foundry D. Stempel AG for Linotype.

ABOUT PHOENICIA PUBLISHING

Phoenicia Publishing is an independent press based in Montreal but involved, through a network of online connections, with writers and artists all over the world. We are interested in words and images that illuminate culture, spirit, and the human experience. A particular focus is on writing and art about travel between cultures—whether literally, through lives of refugees, immigrants, and travelers, or more metaphorically and philosophically—with the goal of enlarging our understanding of one another through universal and particular experiences of change, displacement, disconnection, assimilation, sorrow, gratitude, longing and hope.

We are committed to the innovative use of the web and digital technology in all aspects of publishing and distribution, and to making high-quality works available that might not be viable for larger publishers. We work closely with our authors, and are pleased to be able to offer them a greater share of royalties than is normally possible.

Your support of this endeavor is greatly appreciated.

Our complete catalogue is online at www.phoeniciapublishing.com, where readers can also subscribe to our quarterly newsletter.

BY THE SAME AUTHOR

70 Faces: Torah Poems
by Rachel Barenblat

Phoenicia Publishing is proud to publish this collection of contemporary spiritual writing: poems written in response to the Torah in the longstanding tradition of midrash, by a gifted writer, teacher, and spiritual leader who brings to her work not only deep thought on spiritual life and belief, but the experiences of daily life and society that we all share in the 21st century. In keeping with our cross-cultural focus at Phoenicia, we are certain that *70 Faces* will appeal not only to Jewish readers but all "children of Abraham," as well as those who come to these texts with serious questions, enlarging our understanding and deepening our own thought about a body of writing that lies at the root of the Abrahamic religions, and of western literature.

Each of the poems in *70 Faces* arose in conversation with the Five Books of Moses. These poems interrogate, explore, and lovingly respond to Torah texts - the uplifting parts alongside the passages which may challenge contemporary liberal theology. Here are responses to the familiar tales of Genesis, the liberation story of Exodus, the priestly details of Leviticus, the desert wisdom of Numbers, and the anticipation of Deuteronomy. These poems balance feminism with respect for classical traditions of interpretation. They enrich any (re)reading of the Bible, and will inspire readers to their own new responses to these familiar texts.

—

"In the poetry of 70 Faces, *Rachel Barenblat continues the work of translation and commentary that has occupied her for years as the Velveteen Rabbi. She is as young as our century and as old as Judaism. Her poems have the classic cadence of the scriptures and the fresh wonder of a new mother. These are old words for the modern mind. This is ancient wisdom we can feel and know."*

Pastor Gordon Atkinson,
author of RealLivePreacher.com and *Turtles All The Way Down*

Waiting to Unfold
by Rachel Barenblat

Waiting to Unfold offers an unflinching and honest look at the challenges and blessings of early parenthood.

Poet and rabbi Rachel Barenblat wrote one poem during each week of her son's first year of life, chronicling the wonder and the delight along with the pain of learning to nurse, the exhaustion of sleep deprivation, and the dark descent into -- and eventual ascent out of -- postpartum depression.

Barenblat brings her rabbinic training and deep spirituality to bear on this quintessential human experience. She also resists sentimentality or rosy soft-focus. While some of these are poems of wonder, others were written in the trenches.

These poems resist and refute the notion that anyone who doesn't savor every instant of exalted motherhood deserves stigma and shame. And they uncover the sweetness folded in with the bitter.

—

By turns serious and funny, aching and transcendent, these poems take an unflinching look at one woman's experience of becoming a mother.

These rich poems will carry you into the great timeless miracle and mystery of unfolding littleness, nonstop maternal alertness, beauty and exhaustion and amazing, exquisite tenderness, oh yes.

--Naomi Shihab Nye, author of *Fuel* and *The Words Under the Words*

Annunciation
Sixteen Contemporary Poets Consider Mary

Poetry by
Ivy Alvarez, Rachel Barenblat, Jeanne Marie Beaumont, Kristin Berkey-Abbott,
Chana Bloch, Leila Chatti, Luisa A. Igloria, Mohja Kahf, Vivian Lewin, Vinicius
de Moraes (Natalie d'Arbeloff, trans.), Roderick Robinson, Nic Sebastian, Claudia
Serea, Purvi Shah, Rosemary Starace, and Marly Youmans

Illustrated and Edited by
Elizabeth Adams

A beautiful book that's more human and personal than religious, in which the
enigmatic and universal figure of Mary helps us find common ground.

Phoenicia editor Elizabeth Adams invited a diverse group of poets - Christian,
Muslim, Jewish, Hindu, and secular; mostly but not all female - to consider the
story of Mary and the angel Gabriel for an illustrated collection. She wrote:

*"The annunciation story is a complicated foundational story in western culture.
Patriarchies have used Mary as a model for ideal female acceptance, faith, and
submission to authority, while at the same time millions of people have identified with
her courage, suffering, and patience, and accorded her their personal devotion and deep
respect. I suspect that if we look closely, most of us may have been touched by her story in
some way. I want to encourage you to look at the annunciation from a modern point of
view, as contemporary poets of different cultural backgrounds. Your work can be religious
or secular, traditional or decidedly not, written in a feminist light, a current-events
light, a personal light. I'm not looking for any particular type of thrust or interpretation,
but rather a broad range of responses to this story and this person we know as Mary. I
want to encourage you to think deeply and fearlessly, and to write from your hearts."*

The result of this invitation is a volume filled with creative, surprising, moving,
modern and personal poetic responses to the Annunciation story, with illustrations
from original linocut relief prints made for this book, published in a beautiful
edition with a generous page size, and careful attention to materials and typography.
Your purchase will also directly help present-day women, with 10% of the proceeds
going to refugee relief.

www.ingramcontent.com/pod-product-compliance
Lightning Source LLC
Chambersburg PA
CBHW022036090426
42741CB00007B/1087